Auto Body 5S Sustainment Schedule

Start Date: ____________________ Work Area: ____________________

Person Responsible	Specific Location	Frequency of Activity	Activities to Perform

Auto Body 5S Sustainment Schedule

Start Date: ____________________   Work Area:____________________

Person Responsible	Specific Location	Frequency of Activity	Activities to Perform

Auto Body 5S Sustainment Schedule

Start Date: ____________________ Work Area: ____________________

Person Responsible	Specific Location	Frequency of Activity	Activities to Perform

Auto Body 5S Sustainment Schedule

Start Date: ____________________ Work Area: ____________________

Person Responsible	Specific Location	Frequency of Activity	Activities to Perform

Auto Body 5S Sustainment Schedule

Start Date: ____________________ Work Area: ____________________

Person Responsible	Specific Location	Frequency of Activity	Activities to Perform

Auto Body 5S Sustainment Schedule

Start Date: ____________________ Work Area: ____________________

Person Responsible	Specific Location	Frequency of Activity	Activities to Perform

Auto Body 5S Sustainment Schedule

Start Date: ____________________ Work Area: ____________________

Person Responsible	Specific Location	Frequency of Activity	Activities to Perform

Auto Body 5S Sustainment Schedule

Start Date: ____________________ Work Area: ____________________

Person Responsible	Specific Location	Frequency of Activity	Activities to Perform

Auto Body 5S Sustainment Schedule

Start Date: ____________________ Work Area: ____________________

Person Responsible	Specific Location	Frequency of Activity	Activities to Perform

Auto Body 5S Sustainment Schedule

Start Date: ____________________ Work Area: ____________________

Person Responsible	Specific Location	Frequency of Activity	Activities to Perform

Auto Body 5S Sustainm nt Schedule

Start Date: ____________________ Work Area: ______________________

Person Responsible	Specific Location	Frequency of Activity	Activities to Perform

Auto Body 5S Sustainm nt Schedule

Start Date: ____________________ Work Area: ____________________

Person Responsible	Specific Location	Frequency of Activity	Activities to Perform

Auto Body 5S Sustainment Schedule

Start Date: ____________________ Work Area: ____________________

Person Responsible	Specific Location	Frequency of Activity	Activities to Perform

Auto Body 5S Sust inm nt Sch dul

Start Date: ____________________ Work Area: ____________________

Person Responsible	Specific Location	Frequency of Activity	Activities to Perform

Auto Body 5S Sustainment Schedule

Start Date: ____________________ Work Area: ____________________

Person Responsible	Specific Location	Frequency of Activity	Activities to Perform

Auto Body 5S Sustainment Schedule

Start Date: ____________________ Work Area: ____________________

Person Responsible	Specific Location	Frequency of Activity	Activities to Perform

Auto Body **5S Sustainment Schedule**

Start Date: ____________________ Work Area: ____________________

Person Responsible	Specific Location	Frequency of Activity	Activities to Perform

Auto Body 5S Sustainment Schedule

Start Date: ____________________ Work Area: ____________________

Person Responsible	Specific Location	Frequency of Activity	Activities to Perform

Auto Body 5S Sustainm nt Schedule

Start Date: ____________________ Work Area: ____________________

Person Responsible	Specific Location	Frequency of Activity	Activities to Perform

Auto Body 5S Sustainment Schedule

Start Date: ____________________ Work Area: ____________________

Person Responsible	Specific Location	Frequency of Activity	Activities to Perform

Auto Body 5S Sustainment Schedule

Start Date: ____________________ Work Area: ____________________

Person Responsible	Specific Location	Frequency of Activity	Activities to Perform

Auto Body 5S Sustainment Schedule

Start Date: ____________________ Work Area: ____________________

Person Responsible	Specific Location	Frequency of Activity	Activities to Perform

Auto Body 5S Sustainment Schedule

Start Date: ____________________ Work Area: ____________________

Person Responsible	Specific Location	Frequency of Activity	Activities to Perform

Auto Body 5S Sustainment Schedule

Start Date: ____________________ Work Area: ____________________

Person Responsible	Specific Location	Frequency of Activity	Activities to Perform

Auto Body 5S Sustainment Schedule

Start Date: ____________________ Work Area: ____________________

Person Responsible	Specific Location	Frequency of Activity	Activities to Perform